To Veronica

FREEDOM KNOWS

MY NAME

Be Free!

Kelly Harris-DeBerry

Kelly H

Freedom Knows My Name

Kelly Harris-DeBerry
Copyright © 2020 by Xavier Review Press

Cover design by Justin Batiste
Book design by Bill Lavender

ISBN 978-1883275297

Xavier Review Press thanks the Xavier University Endowment for the Humanities for its support.

For more information, please visit www.xavierreview.com

Scan Me
to listen to a FREE
audio book at
kellyhd.com

Contents

For my parents who shaped me as a poet

For Jarvis and Naomi, all my love—forever

The poet's task is to turn words into song, utter incantations that heal, inspire, be more than ordinary talk. Be the abracadabra that opens us to the fullest appreciation of life, light and love. The fierceness that defends the sacredness of our very existence. No simple occupation. Read. Listen to Kelly. Immediately you know. Her poems are as close as we humans can come to reaching the angelic state. Many of us can write, but only a few of us can truly poet. Ultimately, what we learn from her is that we are alive and capable of astonishing beauty even as we trudge on the treadmills of survival, dealing with the daily trials and tribulations we all to one degree or another must confront. Listen. Behold. A poet speaks to the heart of each of us, celebrates the best of all of us. Articulates the acme, the zenith of human endeavor. The poet. She is the sound of wonderful.

—KALAMU YA SALAAM

Who Will You Say You Are

On that day
when flashlights search
  the hallways of mouths,
the birthplace of our tongues
  for legitimate breath—
American scent?
  What is this burning
of democracy blowing smoke
  in our gullible eyes?
Who will you say you are
in human language?
  Who is worthy
of homes and prayers
and bulletproof churches?
  Could it be you
were born to a God
  with a target on its back
mistaken for Black?
Who passes skin
  like bread baskets?
Who stays overnight
  in America's bed?
Who is this stripper
  with nipples like bombs
calling herself Liberty,
  eating tacos on Tuesdays
  feeding caged children?
  Who will you say deserves

work and government
 and cold water to drink?
Virtual. Virtuous. Vile.
 Who is spooning
the truth to the babies
 with serious eyes
in graveyard schools?
 Whose life is on
the V.I.P survival list?
 Who are you
in the history of now
 when face to face
with matter-of- fact evil
 wearing lab coats
firing government needles
 in your city's arm?
Are you homesick yet?
 Will it be you locked out
from medicine and daylight
wondering if your bones
will be eaten or blessed?
 In the days of left
and left over, who
 will you say you are
when sirens flash,
 buildings crumble?
And you hear
 familiar feet walking
on the world like a gorilla?

"The emotional, sexual, and psychological stereotyping of females begins when the doctor says, 'It's a girl.'"

— SHIRLEY CHISHOLM

It's a Girl

        and girl, let me tell you:
how people wanted you a boy
to carry your father's name.
The running joke is: boys are easier
to straighten out than boy-crazy girls.
Poor dad, they said, rubbing his back
as if you are the pain coming up his legs.
Keep trying for a boy,
a junior, a son—every man wants one—
to shine like a car, keep pace with the globe
of men racing to show off their flags in the Earth.
And it's the women too —
with wives' tales for making boys
and satisfied men— hurry
deliver that man a boy,
as if i should return you like a shirt
or toaster, pop out a different ball of human
oh, girl,
        they would have made you an asterisk,
put me to work on my back again
just to see a boy win.

Due in September

when the baby comes
let it not be

on the same day
the nation

remembers
its blood

like a mother
looking between

her towers
at a tiny human

falling.

I, too,
am a country,

the land
of all bones

pulling bodies
out my soil

welcoming
travelers

from lovers
and dark places

of history
and muted songs

under every sky
is a law,

a lynching
that watched

men smolder
in trees

and gathered
no rain

if there is ash,
no monuments

shall be made
of me

if there is blood,
I want it all

to birth
as I please.

God bless the child
that's got his own

mother,
flag.

September 15

you
    came down
my warm slide
grabbing at cords of air
    as if opening blinds
looking out at life

After Birth

cry   in the bathroom
while others oooh & aaah
over a baby   that does not know
she loves you yet   cry
when visitors   leave you alone
cry   reading the mail   cooking the rice
washing the bottles   scrubbing the skillet
changing the diapers   in the morning
when you want a shower   you cry
at every moment   you thought   was yours
hungry   to taste a break   you cry   barefoot
on the scale   no snap- back body   irrational
crying   who is the baby   crying
to go   somewhere   crying
when it's time to leave   return to   work   crying
over   all the work   pumping milk   crying
over spilled milk   wiping tears
the baby is crying   watching   mother   crying

Miscarriage

the dot
was death
did not know
the dot
was death
did not feel
the dying
coming
did not know
a funeral
was arriving
between
my legs
did not know
this blood came
to kill
did not know
death could be
so quiet
did not know
a baby
was dying
did not know
a baby was living
did not know
the baby was mine

did not know
how to walk
back into life
empty

If I went to a therapist, I would say

The life
that brought me
here

is not worth telling.
Weren't you raised
to never tattle?

or cry long?
If you fall,
riding a bike

twist a knee,
ignore the blood.
Try again,

is how you survive
the Midwest:
work hard

without looking back.
Who has time to lie
on a couch and pay

for questions
I've asked myself
when feeling lost?

But then again,
I never ask directions.
Where I'm from

never know who's
carrying concern
like a knife.

Watch the person
spinning the chair.
There is no sitting

or crying to strangers
there's work to do.
Since fourteen,

I've paid bills
passed down in my name,
adulthood on credit.

All the chores of shame
I've done to keep a roof
over my head and mouth.

My life's throat—
a long tunnel of sorrow.
Tell me,

what do you see
down there?
Tell me

what I swallowed
that turned off
the light.

Weird, Am I?

for Naomi

How could they know
the word for your light

or what a human can do?
Anyone can string

the alphabet together,
make you laughable,

hold two fingers
behind your head.

You are not alien
Orbiting their planets

I wish you
antennas and

a small voice
in your head beyond

the universe
of your school days.

Imagine yourself

outrunning all the laughter
chasing you

and throwing it in the air
like confetti

or whatever 2nd graders throw
when happiness is in their hands.

Who knows
if you're "good weird"

or bad weird.
Could be you,

most worthy.
Wonderful—

called out
its name.

Mama say

Mama say
Mama say
she ain't no slave
Mama say
Mama say
she ain't no maid
Mama say
Mama say
eat her food
Mama say
Mama
didn't raise no fool
Mama say
Mama say
betta love me now
Mama say
soon Mama
won't be
around

...And the Joke's on Us

black mama:

      the world's piñata

swing   low and laugh high

break her   insides

gather   the pieces of our mamas

           auction them to the highest

black
       laugh

           lash

yo mama so broke(n)

      away   from love
daddy
     ain't never   the joke
       a   ghost gone

never   close   enough

to hurt   back

           laugh at

For Church Girls Forced to Apologize

In many churches, especially black congregations, if an unmarried girl or woman became pregnant, she was made to repent to the congregation. This practice has become less popular over the years but is still common.

church girls
  in off-white

dresses

appropriately
      sorry

ritually
  embarrassed

standing
in a garden,

bitten for the whole
world
    to see

but where is he
      that came

and slithered
away

with the other
half of

the apple?

Ex

he tells me
I'll regret this day
scratch his door like a cat
says epiphany will knock me
to my knees
I'll be right there, looking up,
thanking God

"i survive on intimacy & tomorrow..."

—NTOZAKE SHANGE

For the Women Who Save Me

and pull me up for air
covering me in blankets of honey

setting my table with a vase of mirth
bringing fruit baskets and soup

to the lips of my children.
They come through doors

made from long-ago intuition,
daughtering me like their own.

The women come knowing
the scent of hard times

grating worry into bowls
shaping meals by hand.

The women come ready,
washing loads of my business

folding me back into place.
These women, stiff lovers

demand my sorrows
on polished silver.

They come, disciples
of their mothers

grandmothers
field workers,

shucking tears
like corn.

Pressing my hard head
into pearl.

The women come,
in the rain, after work,

in the midnight,
to rock my regret to sleep.

They come, fussy,
and broken, washing

my face with compassion,
patching my heartbreak

with laughter.
Guarding my name

with candlelight.
They come barefoot,

conjuring ancestors
with Yoruba songs

and oiled blessings.
The women come

in dreams and flesh
like pregnant armies

loaded with grenades of love
and sharp warm eyes

filled with visions of women
saving themselves.

Grown Women Conversations

rise from pews of women
testifying in the salon.
A halo of cuss words
and hot comb smoke
crowned my tender head.
I sat on a stack of books
in a chair made
for a woman's hurt.

There were two kinds of men:
no count, hard working—
their names, even kinfolk,
cut to the floor.

First time I heard trifling,
I knew it was a man
wasting a woman's love.
Choose wisely, they said:
"Once a man gets in yo head,
your thighs do all the thinking."

They sat long to be beautiful
set their tears to dry.
Coded words like:
"banana" for men's parts
"headache" for no sex
"couch" for almost divorced.

I've seen it all:
flames striking lovers,
clothes thrown from porches
teams of women resisting
one man's bended-knee apology.

I leaned into thick love stories
and quick neck rolls.
All the women,
a long braid of beauty,
all their hands
trimming dead ends.

Advice to Newlyweds

if you want to stay in love,
                    say I'm sorry

if you want to stay married,
                    say I was wrong

Ms. Edna

New Orleans

Believe everything a man say
he sell air and they buy

All his words, all the diapers
baby, after baby, after baby

No husband or piece of a man
tell me how such pretty ladies hook

with day-old-bread-looking-niggas
can't walk straight, pants too big—

Wish somebody beat they little ass
stank ain't familiar to their own children

Ooooh, my father's feet was rotten,
but I knew he was there

And ladies, fix ya selves. Quick yo mind.
Don't be no man's house fly or sexy dummy.

Stash some dollars in ya bra.
Cook with big pots if ya can. I'll teach ya.

By nineteen, I made pound cake, gumbo,
yeast rolls, peach cobbler—all from scratch

yes, I did. My sweetness was trouble.
All my folks ever told me was don't kiss

a boy, you'll get pregnant. So I didn't kiss,
but I did everything else.

Women Listening to Acclaimed Poet

Say she a poet
But I don't understand
How words come out
with no place to land
Didn't think words
could turn up their nose
but I guess they do
All the people clapping
but I'm dozing on you

"It was like sewing ruffles on a fence of nails. The will to make life beautiful was so strong."

—Zora Neale Hurston

Migration. My Family. My Cleveland.

Left
       your land
  for a job,

the same Southern job,

the always job of
          surviving white folks.

Working hard ain't never impressed them.

      Why a farmer like you go North?

The land is hitched to steel
      and tight-lipped mornings

No elbow room for joy
      No time to rock the Earth asleep

Had a porch, a pulpit then,
     stories sprouted from dirt and spirit

Here ain't by the riverside
     don't flow back to ancient gospels.

God is a check here,
     a blue collar, a few days off

Remember those clock-less days,
        when soil called you to work

I reckon it's worth leaving the land
        if heaven is up, away from cotton,

away from the wrong white people
            hoping to find the right ones.

Maybe,
    up there, Klan fires fade in rear view,
    trees dangle the weight of snow

How'd you learned to live
        in the cold and rude and disrespect?

They don't sip nothing sweet up here.
They lynch us slow, over time
    brick by brick into heavy-breathers
    of smoke, polite anger.

I weep

for all the times
    the Navy called you boy

all the middle fingers
    you should have raised

all the labor,
   half the paycheck

all the white flight
   that left big city rats

eating the floorboards
   nailed from your knees

Your blood in the wood.
   Your blood in the would have been

I live the same two-step blues
   of kinfolk made in the Delta

Integrated with white children
   whose parents were the white people
that niggered you

How many miles did you travel
   to be more than fractions of dreams

Grandpa, did you ever
   cross the Dixie again in your sleep?

Did you ever bring America home?

Names Don't Name Me

My 6th graders know
good words from bad ones,
except when the word
starts with N.
Sometimes it's hard for them
to explain why
it drifts easy without an anchor
or thought or history
or excuse me or oops
or don't or stop saying
that N word.
It's just there, they say—
on purpose sometimes,
a habit mostly between
friends, ya know?
The N word don't mean
what it meant.
Used to be a bad sign
in a yard, on fire in the South.
It's just familiar talk before
what's up or please.
It's the beat we speak
when the radio's on
and the jokes fly.
It's the punch line
emphasized. You've heard

a woman cussing mad
or a fight starting in a street
Could be a N word
acting like an N.
Depends,
on the mouth's
meaning and if
you're in or outside
of strangers (white folks).
Don't want them
thinking our talk
is theirs, it's different.
Can't explain why
our English
don't mean—mean
the way it used to
in slavery, in Mississippi,
in Georgia, in Memphis,
in Kentucky, in stores,
in bathrooms, in schools,
in courtrooms, in elections
in hospitals, in restaurants,
in banks, in day or night.
The N word don't hang
on doors or trees
or chase my feet or grandpa
no more. That's history, they say.
6th graders know these things.

They learned it all before
knowing the right way
to rub words together
to start a fire.

The Way it Was

waaay back
before we were urban
on subways standing freestyle
sinking battleships
pulling rhymes from
the crack of our hips
dissed yo mama's mama
for wearing church shoes
and jogging pants
posed on the corner
in a B-boy stance
on one knee
Soul Train linked
hands on booties
at the roller rink
me myself and i
plus the homies
all wanted to be Theo
mama never let us go
past streetlights
or without Christmas
every week
girls double dutched
as boys nodded to their breast beat
sweet softness in motion
like snare buckets
on New York streets

always inspired a nickname
a new way to spit game
or vocab flow
couldn't decide between
Atari or turntables
stole vinyl from my auntie's milk crate
made my cousin swear by
the soul brother handshake
to never rat
when i came home too late
at the break of dawn
when the party stopped
there was still the boom box
on brown shoulders
carrying us the way our music
does on rent day
it be thick like that
heavy sometimes
shoved in our backpack
like Superman
we just be flying off at the mouth
to make sense of the edge
between cutting and breaks
we danced and walked
like Radio Raheem
keeping the ghetto condition cool
during police heat
the soreness in the sound

cleared the throat to speak
we walked the beat
there were no platinum nooses then
we were just
                    hanging

Push it and see what happens

after Salt-N-Pepa

Never
could I moan,
  Oooh, baby, baby
like those fleshy women
  rolling their backs
into breathlessness.
  Under this roof,
there was God watching
  my mother watching me.
Lovers dance but not
  in girls' bodies.
My parents,
  a one-way door,
the Jesus way,
  sealed the music shut
  against boys and babies
coming too soon.
  A girl's reputation
feathers her future.
  I was not going
to be a fast-tail girl
  with a leather attitude
back talking in red lipstick
  and jungle earrings.
All the wild
  I could have been

never left my body.
  House rules always chained
around my neck
— heavier than gold.

For Bender Ave. Girls

East Cleveland

Chalked names on concrete squares
warn the world:
        step to us with a bouquet
of respect. We live here, too,
among blades of boys
and broken classroom windows,
after school, the smell of urine
and flirty men fill the streets.
        Fast girls cause we gotta be,
moving like a unit of soldiers,
ready to pull knives, jump ropes
and fences—shooing dogs silent.
We stilt walk above factory smoke,
braid our hair like a Mary J album.
Our laughter, loud and lonely—eligible
for living on blocks where cheese and children
get chopped into sections of eight.
        Kinfolk tell stories in kitchens
of Alabama and burning crosses.
We daughters of daughters of runaway
Negroes still bent in the fields of yesterday.
Maps of our mothers veined in our palms,
We catch buses and side-eyes while searching
for the same North star that brought us here.
We survive like every bad mayor elected,
pretend our tears are hard laughs.

Word on the street is
our bodies flow easy. No daddies
stand guard, but we cross our arms
into black girl stance under streets lights
popping gum like warning shots.

Reverend Wagner's House

East Cleveland

Wild rainbow of a house.
Crazy Nigga, some say.
Heard God and magic snakes
lived there. I witnessed
the Reverend slanted
in a twin bed, a landscape of genius,
mouth like a cursive O.
Otherworld Black.
A Sun Ra kinda prayer.
No telling what planet
Rev. was on—
it was all a zigzag,
a petting zoo of philosophies.
You are a bowling ball,
with three eyes, he said.
Mind. Body. Spirit.
Head toward the devils
leave none standing.

Shaw High School Mighty Cardinals

East Cleveland

Like ants in uniform

    black legs marched a maze of music.
From porches and curbs

    we watched all the neighborhood kids
line up carefully like dominoes.

    Mothers calling
their child through megaphoned hands:

    Lil Bump was the smallest
big head behind a tuba.
                Gone boy!
    Tasha
twirled everythang
              forbidden.
   All of them,
proof we were more than ghetto
            more than bullets

All that red on their bodies
            was not blood.

Super Sunday: New Orleans

Black people, ordinary royalty
 crown themselves
  in boldface streets
 tip their heads back
into unpredictable skies.
Dance between bad days & bright feathers.
 Gold teeth, sweaty women, squat low
    and nest on this unbreakable city.
Burdens laid down
 under the bridge, on a porch, on a rooftop—
 is how you fly away
  for a moment, a lifetime.
Trumpets and trombones point
back at God.
    This is the sound of the people
who came through bloody waters
afloat on faith and ancient drums
dancing to remember
  how to unchain the body;
return it to a sea of freedom.
   Look at this Sunday,
unspeakable joy—
   all the glory,
     all the footwork.

A Lesson on Land

you are never too young
to prepare for enemies

trust me,

    one day
this will be you on a square

facing men like wildfires

and you will remember
this chess game

my voice dragging your hand
to the place of our plow

your great-grandparents
lined up in the wind

whispering: this is your land

        unmovable

Strangers Looking to Buy My House (That's Not for Sale)

Trust Fund Baby Way

Used to Be Black Blvd.

White Flight Returned Exchange

they don't ask
they don't knock
they drive down
your block
to see what you got

corporate biz
non-profit-pimps
tourist trips

they measure your grass
move in fast
by the time that you look
it's already took

they come for the culture
take it all over
make you a stranger
displace all your neighbors

erase what you had
make it brand new
upscale all the food
appropriate you

sell all of the
schools
cheat on the scores
blame all the kids

they don't ask
they don't knock
they drive down your block

Millennial Coffee Shop Avenue

60

Trust Fund Baby Way

Rent Too Damn High St.

Rich them, Poor Us Blvd.

to see what you got
by the time that you look
it's already took

call it organic
say it's for good

they don't ask
they don't knock
they drive down your
block

to see what you got
by the time that you look
it's already took

hide the oppression
then call it progression

who is it
who is it

savior complex
inner city checks
grant statistics
police at my door
for looking suspicious

knock
knock
who is it

who?

Millennial Coffee Shop Avenue

"

"Choose your leaders with wisdom and forethought.
To be led by a coward is to be controlled by all that the coward fears.
To be led by a fool is to be led by the opportunists who control the fool.
To be led by a thief is to offer up your most precious treasures to be stolen.
To be led by a liar is to ask to be told lies.
To be led by a tyrant is to sell yourself and those you love into slavery."

— OCTAVIA BUTLER, *Parable of the Talents*

53%

believe
America
is for women
white enough
to think like
a man

Mrs. Potato Head

Rachel Dolezal

Rachel
Rachel

Potato
potahto

African-American
black

ID
person

Feel it
fake it

Mrs.
potato

Head
brown

Body
make it

Tan
darker

Than
DNA

Hey
ain't you

Her
theirs

No
not really

Nappy
hair

Braided
twisted

Colored
over

Until
color

Matches
them

Full lips
thick hips

Learned
it

Stole it
sued

Howard
how

To
learn

Blackness
study

Women
mothers

Sistas
angry

Deep
artist

Types
needed

Sons
for reporting

Police
to prove

Pain
is really

Black
pain

Performance
needed

Proof
a look

An image
to be

Down
girl,

You go
made us

look
N
A
A
C
P

Head
potato

Parts
poked

Pinned
blackness

On
herself

Made
blackness

Trans
not

Trans
Atlantic

Boat
booty

Nah
accessories

Decorate
decode

Fantasy
black father

Wishes
blew out

Whiteness
cake

Walk
privilege

Pass
passed

Sandra
Bland

Reheisha
McBride

Rachel
never

Died
lied

Pieces
parts

Rearrange
mrs.

Potato
new

Race
game

Wanna be
lifelike

Civil rights
handshake

Mistake
erase

Black
women

Again &
again

Until
black

Men
say

White
oppression

Was
good

Intention
con/sequence

Con/sciousness
con artist

We
believed

Never questioned
reality

Frontin
in front

Of the
world

White girl
put black

Bodies
on

Black bodies
don't

Get put
on

Jobs
tv

Book
deals

White
puppetry

Hands up
our

Black
narration

Victimization
racism

Classification
check

How much
is her

Check
zeroes

Negroes
ain't

Chunks
of memory

Mrs. Potato
embellishment

White
imagination

Integration
imitation

Flattery
not

Smiling
black lives

White lies
Hidden inside

White bodies
Black lives

White lies
hidden inside

White
bodies

History of the P word in Donald, USA

Palefaces
Populate
Plantations
        that's how they grab it

Power
Possesses
Properties
        that's how they grab it

Prejudice
Perpetuates
Pipelines

        that's how they grab it

Police
Poor People's
Progress

        that's how they grab it

Poverty
Prohibits
Progress

        that's how they grab it

Privileged
Predators
Pollute

     that's how they grab it

Partners
Preserve
Petroleum

     that's how they grab it

Preparing
Poisonous
Panic

     that's how they grab it

Programming
Porn
Patriotism

     that's how they grab it

Pimps
Poison
Pandemonium

     that's how they grab it

Prescribe
Phony
Prescriptions

       that's how they grab it

Pacify
Public
Participation

       that's how they grab it

Permit
Psycho
Presidents

       that's how they grab it

Oil

Oil depends on us
Oil depends on us for money
how much   depends on   us
oil on us   oil on us
oil on us   depends on money for us
oil makes   money   for more
oil   to go   go
            go on   depend on money   won't be
enough   for us   enough for us
enough!   oil   money
makes us   money makes us   more
                    oil makes us need more oil
us needs more   money   to make
how much   depends on how much
us   us   us   us

Do The Lies Matter

do they lie   do they lie down
            together
one government
            same president
playing   dress up as God
who's the shadow
            who's the   savior
who's gonna   save us
            from being sheep
voters   are trophies   in the hands
            of a grinning democracy
with a sweet tooth for lies   wars
            &   ham sandwiches
what's in the meat   of human swine
            does it matter
who's getting milked with   cookies
            & evangelical panic
what's for sale   who bought
            the White House
            & paid with our children
sold us   to a hell   that tastes so good
            we ask for more
hashtags   imprisonment
            behind the screen
copied & pasted   pretending   trending

             filtered humanity
snap-out-of-it   boxed   tagged
             you're it,
what's   the   matter   with   you?

American Junkie

America
needs a smoke

that lynched-body smoke

it's addictive   America
needs that hit
                of brutality

it's addictive
                needs Whiteness
                up its nose

sniffs the ballot
licks the Constitution
itches for power

until it is the high(est)
                hierarchy

                so addictive

    we think we want
                their power

but what we really need

                is freedom.

"Like a lot of Black women, I have always had to invent the power my freedom requires."

—JUNE JORDAN

What She Should Have Said

for Anita Hill

In a voice mail message left at 7:31 a.m. on Oct. 9, 2001, Virginia Thomas asked Anita Hill to consider apologizing for testifying against her husband, Clarence Thomas, during his 1991 Supreme Court confirmation hearings.

Most days I hold my tongue until I am water—
but today,
   I am 'Nita—
dropping the "A" off to ass whup
like the angry Black woman you imagine
hiding inside a bear.
    I have dreamed of growling,
shredding my dress, chasing whiteness
with a machete off a steep cliff—
Countless times, I've come home to myself,
leaving my shoes and anger at the door.

In my world, I fetch no water
for the lies of your lips. I work in the cool
of my freedom. Ms. Thomas, where is the blood
on your so-called lynching tree?
Where is the terror upon your endless face?
All that unnecessary blushing,
I hope you pray about it.

What Separates Us (In the Voice of Demetrie McLorn)

"The only time I ever saw Demetrie out of her white uniform was when she was in the casket." Kathryn Stockett, author of "The Help," in a March 2, 2010, interview with Katie Couric. Demetrie was Stockett's grandmother's maid for 32 years and died when Stockett was age 16.

I.

White folks
got their own
commandments.

Even their children
demand cold drinks
by my first name.
Feel like a nigger doll

when they cry at me to play
with their fingers and shadows.
I touch white children carefully

as if they were glass.
Mornings, I pin whites to clothes lines
and see no heaven.
I tie my apron into half-smiles,

agree with their barren laughter.
I don't taste the joy
forced into my mouth.

I want to slice a slither of goodness.
Carve myself new. Imagine me
free—sitting at noon teas
pouring out my Negro self;

clinking with the company.
Oh, how I wish
you a day's work in Magnolia heat,
in the Colored Section.

Yes, Ma'am, I can teach you how to smile
and hold your nose in a room full of bastards.
You stir in sugar while I hold rage behind
the jail of my teeth.

2.
I was dead the moment
I needed your permission
to smell God's flowers.

What is this mercy
you've given to me
that keeps me enslaved?

Like family,
That's what you call me
as if you know the difference
between the warmth of my face
and a cast iron skillet.

You white folks sho do tell stories
with leaky truths. But I know
if you were up here,

You'd assign me the last row in heaven.
If you wished me back
your feet still be in front of mine,
law still be your best friend

pay still be overdue
worry still set my table
beauty still be White Only

and I'd still have one good dress.

How Fast Must She Run

for Serena Williams

**In 2015 Serena Williams became the first black
woman to win Sports Illustrated's Sportsperson of the
Year. The other finalist for the prize: thoroughbred
racehorse: American Pharaoh.*

and they're off   America   ahead
Serena on the outside

American Pharaoh, a horse of course
four feet   vs.   two

the grandstand sips bourbon
in seersuckers & straw hats

fanning the heat of Southern memory
when it was   Only Them   only

plantation   country club
always bet on the pleasure of   beating

breeding   horses   slaves
slap skin into speed   watch cotton

grow   pick   pick
the fastest pedigree

White men   get free rides   chase   black tail
Serena in neon   muscular and

mouthy   grunting   normal   human
Compton   competition   Who taught

her   French tongues
crowd anticipates poor unexpected Black

Serena   more Egyptian   than horse

Serena   still on the outside again   Never
crowned   American

Pharaoh   giddy up   giddy up   giddy up
like police   mounting black bodies on

pavement   How fast must she run
between history & manure?   How fast must she
run?   Between net & noose?

She is a she. Hair in beads.
An abacus on her shoulders

counting the burden of winning
counting the danger of excellence

America's firm lead is a safe bet.
All the race cards checked. Ready.

Cash in.   What stallions America makes.   Breaks
them.   It's a break away

America.   In front, always. Animal-like,
Always. Serena, the speed

of a thousand feet of gold.
This is history. History making Black women

less than animal. The only way to be heard
is to growl. Slam.   Serena

more than skin's distance away now. She's
gaining. More distance to go.

Gaining. More distance to go. America. Overlay.
Serena. Running against time.

Who's keeping time. More distance to go.
Closing in. More distance to go. America.

Serena.

Running. Running. Running...

Sonia

our Sankofa song
returning us to the soil
of our names
  who are we
but a poem traveling
on your tongue
  you open the tombs
of our ancestors
tend to history's back
with a lash of laughter
  only the ocean knows
our pain, the taste
  of stolen blood
you sing us lullabies
in the angry hours
crashing waves of wisdom
against our insanity
  resist, you say,
resist. resist. resist,
  herding us like Harriet's
sacred hands, you are
warm water, black Earth
  mother tongue, speak to us
in righteous volume
  lead us to small discoveries

in our palms
  sober this drunken world
with your full-grown honey
  make us sweet again.

We Will Go to War and Leave You Bloody

"If you the men of Ashanti will not go forward, then we will. We the women will. I shall call upon my fellow women. We will fight the white men. We will fight until the last of us falls in the battlefields."
-Yaa Asantewaa

We have been patient in your kingdom,
made armies from our blood.
The bliss you promised the people
has turned into slaughter.
War blows back upon your silly face.
Your testosterone has failed
and only flirted with freedom.
We are taking the drums back
beating away familiar cowards.
We looked over our bosoms
and see no food or kings.
Our legs will not open for your return.
Remember this lioness look.
Watch us war. Watch us kill.

"I'll tell you what freedom means to me: No fear."

—NINA SIMONE

Hunker Down

because you never know
if the seasons are on speaking terms,
snow could decide to fall
into tantrum in summer.
And then what? Ice skating in June?
Or worse, a tornado whisking cars into your
neighbor's kitchen.
If you hear the sound of trains coming,
my grandmother would say, get ready.
Unexplainable days are coming
to crawl up your skin, empty your pockets.
You'll know by the pain, Earth has lost patience
with hell raisers and robots. You'll know that
train is closer when the zoo becomes the world
with its hands up in desperate prayer.

Our Greatest Weapon

We are dangerous
when we love
When we love
we are dangerous
Dangerous we are
when we love We

Always

my parents will die
and surprise me
at the kitchen sink on the day
when I'm going on without crying
their voices will check the counters
for crumbs and cluttered spices
and food dropped to the floor.
They will walk beside me again,
their rules coming back to my hands
and I will call my daughter back
to finish the chores right the first time.
I won't believe it's them again,
in me, double checking the locks,
every door before dark, then praying
before laying down to sleep.
They will look in on me
from some hall with bright light
and we will watch over our children together

A Meditation on the Duck Boat Accident (July 2018)

Water. The break(ing). The gateway of life.
*

We swam our mother's ocean—a blessed current.
*

Somebody throw me an umbilical cord.
I'm drowning.
*

Motherless.
How do I swim in this sea of strangeness?
*

Where's water taking us?
*

Under
Out
Over
*

Thrown over ships.
So many bodies poured out
of Africa.
*

they made our houses slave ships
they made our houses slave ships
they made our houses slave ships

                    --New Orleans

*

Baptize America
and see if she comes up
less racist. Holy?
*

Water is a Weapon
Water is a Weapon
Water is a Weapon
        --Sincerely,
        Flint, Michigan
*

Black people can't swim is not a joke.
*

My swim instructor says:
Relax.
Let go.
*

Look good by the pool
never get in the pool
can't get hair wet,
nappy.
*

A wet woman
deserves worship.

*

All our black lives
we have been flesh
out of water

out of continent
outsiders
on bloody land.
*
What black fears
keep you from living?
*
It's just water.
*
Woman loses nine family members in Duck Boat
accident.
*
Imagine losing an entire family...
*
Flashback--

Middle Passage:
dead bodies chained to the living

Tallahatchie River:

remember that Chicago boy
that became our son,
our testimony
*
Water is our witness.
*
Water calls our names.

*
Holds our bodies
in our mothers

until she breaks
pouring libation.

May Death Be

for Nikki B.

May the heaven
you prayed for come
out the wondrous nowhere
and take you on a joy ride
at the speed of forever.
May your limbs join constellations
and light my grief.
May your end be
more than fairy tale and gold.
May you wait for me on that promised day
and prove my weeping
wrong.

The Death Between Us

Blood races through plastic tubes
like a marathon runner,
laps of breath,
around unknowable days
We were once lovers
without the moan of machine
and death cracking the door.
From the other side
my hands are folded under my cheek,
a prayer, I guess, to sleepless nights.
I watch the ripple of your chest
to pace your leaving.
Grateful to know death
could look like a fresh grave,
mouth open. One cold kiss away,
I lean into your stillness
and my God you are still warm,
still here.

I tell my daughter: mama and daddy won't always be around

and she says, *fine*
crossing her tantrum arms
stomping away from a God
that does mean things
meant for good
so let's die together,
hold hands under water
and swim to a new blue breath

Casket Dance

in New Orleans,
the gods   blow death
out weeping mouths
until the spirit comes
upon a Black woman
in stilettos
hammering grief
into twilight
dancing the dead's
last   word

Last Words, Last World

We say to the wind,
    we will not speak
    to provoke slaughter

We say to the sun,
    guard our spines

We say to the moon,
    we will prepare
    for midnight

We say to the river,
    carry our egos away

We say to the hills,
    we are not weary

We say to the trees,
    be our cooling shield

We say to the animals,
    we will no longer
    live as wild beasts

We say to the children,
    your Earth is calling

How to Die Like a Diva

for Aretha Franklin

To be eternal
you gotta be extra

gotta stretch death out
around the corner

feed the people
your life

let it linger round
the rim of their lips

you want them talking
remembering

your voice
touching their skin

forever, framed
on living room mantels

and bootleg T-shirts.
every version of you

worn by the neighborhood
ReRe

respect pouring,
liquor on concrete

you ain't nobody
if the city don't cry

and preach your name
Oh, you gotta invite God,

parade scriptures.
Dip back

into old waters
that cleansed sinners

on Sunday mornings.
You must be church

a steeple of a woman
Anthem in flesh

Demanding
a big ole solo

at the world's altar
so no one can stop watching

black ritual grief
go on and on and on

really long
out of order,

over time, CP time,
with no apologies—

going up yonder
must be sacred spectacle,

mega tradition
hats and offerings

ushers awaiting the faint
and salvation moan

Hallelujahs
holy ghost

wholly singer
come, sit

at this gold table
you prepared.

Show 'em how
to love the Lord

and luxury.
Flaunting death

in the faces
of the living

crossing your
precious feet

wearing the devil's
favorite color

entering those
pearly gates

tossing that fur --
and before you sing --

posing for the angels,
ask them,

how do I look?

I Still Believe

for Judy Scott

*"Her son dead and her stupid ass still believing in
Jesus. She dumb af."*
*—Facebook comment on Walter Scott's mother's
statement of faith after the December 2016 mistrial.*

All those underground prayers
used to be good enough
to feed the children—
   warmed Nat Turner's hands.
For you, all the marchers prayed
and grandmas too, in Jesus' name
   O.M.G, ain't that a prayer?
Ain't that how revolutionaries talk
to God now, text it, post it. Posture-less.
But what do you know
  about a dead son
  on a stranger's phone.
You want it all,
everyone's dream on your T-shirts
But you can't have my resurrection.
  Can't tell me there is no God.
My son was in my Earth
in a nine-month grave I could not see.
  Held him on his first bloody day
until he walked

the line back
to me in baby steps.
Ain't no waiting on heaven.
I've seen the afterlife.

Acknowledgments

Poems from this book have appeared in the following journals or publications:

"Names Don't Name Me" in PLUCK Magazine; *"Casket Dance"* in 400yrs: The story of Black people in poems written from love 1619–2019 (Third World Press,); *"The Way it Was"* Words Beats & Life The Global Journal of Hip Hop; *"It's a Girl"* in *Valley Voices*: A Literary Review.

Special thanks to Ralph Adamo and the editorial team at *Xavier Review* for believing in this book and providing incredible patience and support. Thank you to Maurice Ruffin for quietly championing this book. My sincere gratitude to Terri Cross-Davis, *The Langston Hughes Review*, Justin Baptiste, and Kalamu ya Salaam. My deepest gratitude to Freddi Evans, Mimi, Thomas, Ayo, The Lee Family and Shelly for supporting me as a writer and mother to ensure this book would be completed. Special thanks to the village: Christian Unity, Ashe' Cultural Arts Center, Community Book Center and the Cleveland literary community. Gratitude for fellowships at Fine Arts Works Center and Cave Canem.

To Cleveland, the city that is the foundation for

my education, grit, faith and ambition and will
always be home.
To New Orleans, the city that helped shaped my
womanhood joy.

To my parents who always believed my poems
were valuable and ensured I stayed connected
to community and God. To my siblings: Yvette,
Bud, Antoinette and Jocelyn, thank you for all
your support and love. To Naomi, may you always
have courage and know you are loved. To Jarvis,
my husband, friend and toughest reader.